Biblical Hebrew Picture Dictionary

~~~~~~

By Jeff A. Benner

Cover photo by Denise Benner

"Biblical Hebrew Picture Dictionary," by Jeff A. Benner. ISBN 978-1-947532-98-4 (softcover); 978-1-947532-99-1 (eBook).

Published 2018 by Virtualbookworm.com Publishing, P.O. Box 9949, College Station, TX 77842, US. ©2018, Jeff A. Benner. All rights reserved. Any part of this book may be copied for educational purposes only, without prior permission.

All scriptural quotes are from the American Standard Version (ASV) unless otherwise noted. But note that the name "Jehovah" in this translation has been replaced with "YHWH."

This book is dedicated to all my loyal readers and supporters. Without you this book would not have been possible. Thank you.

Contents

Acknowledgments

I would like to thank my wife Denise who not only inspired this book, but also provided the cover photo. I would also like to thank Doris Dippel for her invaluable assistance in editing this document, as well as Wesley B Rose, Ph. D., Philip Gates and Neala Bornman for their excellent suggestions and corrections.

All

כֹּל

Strong's #
3605

kol

And God said, Behold, I have given you <u>every</u> herb yielding seed, which is upon the face of <u>all</u> the earth, and <u>every</u> tree, in which is the fruit of a tree yielding seed; to you it shall be for food: (Genesis 1:29)

This word means "all" and is a very common Biblical Hebrew word appearing over 4,000 times in the Hebrew Bible. The verbal root to this word is *kul* ^(Strong's #3557) and means to sustain in the sense of providing all that is needed for sustenance. For this reason, the word *kol* is related to the verb *akal* ^(Strong's #398) meaning to eat in the sense of sustenance.

Amen

אָמֵן

Strong's #
543

amen

And Benaiah the son of Jehoiada answered the king, and said, <u>Amen</u>: YHWH, the God of my lord the king, say so too. (1 Kings 1:36)

Worldwide this is the most famous of all Hebrew words. But, do we know what it means? This word comes from the root *aman* (Strong's #539), pronounced *ahmahn*, and means to be firmly planted in place as in Isaiah 22:23 which speaks of a "nail fastened to a *secure* place." The noun form, *amen*, pronounced *ahmehn*, is used in the Biblical text by persons who are affirming a statement. In other words, they are saying "I am firmly agreeing with what has been said." The next time we say *amen*, let's think about what we are agreeing to.

Ark

תֵּבָה

Strong's #
8392

teyvah

Make thee an <u>ark</u> of gopher wood; rooms shalt thou make in the <u>ark</u>, and shalt pitch it within and without with pitch. (Genesis 6:14)

In Biblical Hebrew an ark is any floating vessel. Two types of "arks" are found in the Bible, the ark of Noah, a large wooden ship; and the ark of Moses, a floating basket used for holding fish alive, but used for the infant Moses when he was sent out on the Nile river.

Beard

זָקָן   Strong's # 2206   *zaqan*

"that there came men from Shechem, from Shiloh, and from Samaria, even fourscore men, having their <u>beards</u> shaven and their clothes rent, and having cut themselves, with meal-offerings and frankincense in their hand, to bring them to the house of YHWH." (Jeremiah 41:5)

In ancient Hebrew culture a long and white beard was a sign of age, maturity and wisdom. The verb form of this word, *zaqeyn* (Strong's #2204), is the Hebrew meaning "to be old."

Bee

דְּבוֹרָה Strong's # 1682 *devorah*

They compassed me about like <u>bees</u>; They are quenched as the fire of thorns: In the name of YHWH I will cut them off. (Psalm 118:12)

The root of *devorah* is *davar* (Strong's #1696). This root literally means "to arrange in order," usually in the sense of arranging words in an order to make a sentence or to "speak." A colony of bees is insects living in a completely ordered society, hence its connection to the idea of order.

Behold

הִנֵּה   Strong's #
2009   *hiyneyh*

"And the angle of YHWH appeared unto him in a flame of fire out of the midst of a bush: and he looked, and, <u>behold</u>, the bush burned with fire, and the bush was not consumed." (Exodus 3:2)

"Behold" is a common word found in the Bible (1275 times in the KJV) but not really used in our English language today. Being an abstract word, it does not really convey the Hebraicness of the word *hiyneyh*. Every Hebrew word gives a picture of an action and this word is no different. The original Hebraic meaning of *hiyneyh* is best described as one pointing out something important. We would say "Wow, look at that!"

Being

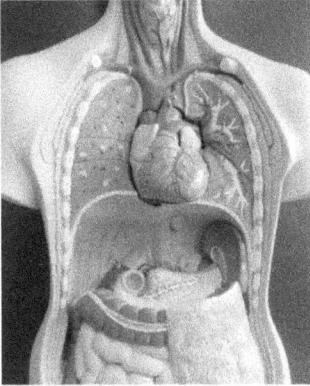

נֶפֶשׁ   Strong's # 5315   *nephesh*

And all the <u>souls</u> that came out of the loins of Jacob were seventy <u>souls</u>: and Joseph was in Egypt already. (Exodus 1:5)

A person is a unity of different parts: the mind, thought, emotion, personality, body, blood, organs, etc. This word is often translated as "soul," implying an abstract entity contained within a person. However, the more Hebraic meaning of this word is "the whole of the person" and can be understood as a "being," "person" or "entity." This word can be used for man (as seen in Genesis 2:7) and animals (as seen in Genesis 1:21 where it usually translated as "creature"). The root of this word, *naphash* (Strong's #5314) means "to refresh" in the sense of restoring the whole of the person to its wholeness through rest and nutrition.

Bird

צִפּוֹר

Strong's #
6833

tsipor

Of all clean <u>birds</u> ye may eat.
(Deuteronomy 14:11)

This Hebrew word is a generic term for all birds. This word is also the name of Tsipor (Romanized as Zippor, Numbers 22:2) and Moses' wife Tsiporah (Romanized as Zipporah, the "ah" is the feminine suffix, Exodus 2:21). The study of "Edenics" looks for connections between Hebrew and other languages. One example of this is the similarity between the Hebrew word *tsipor* (bird) and the word sparrow (a species of bird).

Bless

בָּרַךְ   Strong's # 1288   *barak*

And he made the camels to <u>kneel down</u> without the city by the well of water at the time of evening, the time that women go out to draw water. (Genesis 24:11)

The Hebrew verb *barak* literally means "to kneel." However, when this verb is written in the *piel* form it means "to show respect" (usually translated as "bless"). A related Hebrew word is *berakhah* ^(Strong's #1293), meaning "a gift" or "present." From this we can see the concrete meaning behind the *piel* form of the verb *barak*. It is to present a gift to another while kneeling out of respect. The extended meaning of this word is "to do or give something of value to another." Elohiym "respects" us by providing for our needs and we in turn "respect" Elohiym by giving him of ourselves as his servants.

Box

אָרוֹן   Strong's #
727   *aron*

"And they shall make an <u>ark</u> of acacia wood: two cubits and a half shall be the length thereof, and a cubit and a half the breadth thereof, and a cubit and a half the height thereof." (Exodus 25:10)

There are three "boxes" mentioned in the Hebrew Bible. The *box of the covenant,* usually translated as the *Ark of the Covenant,* contained the objects of the covenant: the manna, Aaron's staff and the tablets. Another box mentioned in the Hebrew Bible is the *box* of Yoseph (Genesis 50:26) or, as most translations translate it, a coffin. The third is identified as a chest in 2 Kings 12:10.

Branch

מַטֶּה

Strong's #
4294

mateh

And YHWH said unto him, What is that in thy hand? And he said, A <u>rod</u>. (Exodus 4:2)

This word is used for the branch of a tree, but is also used for a staff that is a branch cut from a tree; and also for a tribe, as a branch of a family lineage.

Bread

לֶחֶם   Strong's # 3899   *lechem*

"in the sweat of thy face shalt thou eat <u>bread</u>, till thou return unto the ground; for out of it wast thou taken: for dust thou art, and unto dust shalt thou return." (Genesis 3:19)

The dough is placed on the table and kneaded by hitting it with the fists, rolling it back and forth, picking it up and turning it over, and... Kind of sounds like a fight, doesn't it? Actually, the Hebrew noun *lechem* means "bread" and comes from the verbal root *lacham* (Strong's #3898), and means "to fight." The place called Bethlehem is actually two Hebrew words: *beyt* (Strong's #1004) meaning "house" and *lechem* meaning "bread." Together they mean "house of bread." In Genesis 3:19 we read, *In the sweat of your face you shall eat bread.* Could this be because we have to fight (till and weed) the ground to bring up the crop, fight (thresh and winnow) the grain to remove the husk from the seeds, fight (grind) the seeds to turn them into flour and fight (knead) the dough to make the bread?

Brier

שָׁמִיר   Strong's # 8068   *shamiyr*

and I will lay it waste; it shall not be pruned nor hoed; but there shall come up <u>briers</u> and thorns: I will also command the clouds that they rain no rain upon it. (Isaiah 5:6)

Frequently this word is used in the book of Isaiah in the phrase *shamiyr v'shayit* (briers and thorns). This word comes from the root *shamar* (Strong's #8104) often translated as "keep," but more literally meaning "to guard" or "preserve." When a shepherd was out at night with the flock he would construct a corral of briers (*shamiyr*) to "preserve" the flock from predators.

Brother

אָח   Strong's #
        251   *ahh*

And again she bare his <u>brother</u> Abel. And Abel was a keeper of sheep, but Cain was a tiller of the ground. (Genesis 4:2)

The original pictographic script of Hebrew used a picture for each letter. This word would have had the picture of an ox head (*aleph*) representing "strength" and a wall (*hhet*) representing "protection." This Hebrew word (*ahh*) has two meanings. The first is a "hearth," which was a circle of rocks that enclosed the fire to protect and contain it. The second is "the brother." The brothers of the family, like the rocks of the hearth, surrounded the family inside camp to protect it from enemies. Both the rocks of the hearth and the brothers of the family are the "strong protectors."

Camel

גָּמָל

Strong's #
1581

gamal

"behold, the hand of YHWH is upon thy cattle which are in the field, upon the horses, upon the asses, upon the <u>camels</u>, upon the herds, and upon the flocks: there shall be a very grievous murrain." (Exodus 9:3)

The English word camel is from the Greek word *kamelos* which in turn is from the Hebrew word *gamal*. The camel was a common animal in the herds of the nomads of both the ancient and modern times. A nomad's wealth was measured by the size of his herds of livestock including camels (see Genesis 30:43). Camels were a choice beast of burden because of their ability to carry large loads and being able to travel long distances without water.

City

עִיר

Strong's #
5892

iyr

And YHWH came down to see the <u>city</u> and the tower, which the children of men builded. (Genesis 11:5)

Do cities sometime appear as "dark" places? The Ancient Hebrews seemed to think so. The Hebrew parent root *ar* can mean a "city" or an "enemy." Take a look at these other Hebrew words, all with the *ar* root within them. *Ariyph* is a cloud; *sa'ar* is a storm; *arav* is to grow dark; *ur* is blind; *ya'ar* is a forest; *iyr* is a city; *sho'ar* is offensive or vile and *arphel* (origins of awful?) is a thick darkness.

Correctness

צֶדֶק

Strong's #
6664

tsedeq

YHWH ministereth judgment to the peoples: Judge me, O YHWH, according to my <u>righteousness</u>, and to mine integrity that is in me. (Psalm 7:8)

While this word is usually translated as "righteousness," the more concrete Hebraic meaning is "correctness," in the sense of walking in the "correct" path.

Counsel

עֵצָה   Strong's #
6098   *eytsah*

With God is wisdom and might;
He   hath   <u>counsel</u>   and
understanding. (Job 12:13)

The word *eytsah*, meaning counsel, is the feminine form of the masculine word *eyts* (Strong's #6086) meaning "a tree." Counsel is the giving of advice, encouragement or guidance. Within the family or the community this would be from an elder, one filled with years of wisdom and experience. In the Hebrew mind this elder or counselor and his counsel are seen as support to the community in the same way that the trunk of a tree supports the branches of the tree.

Crimson

תּוֹלַעַת   Strong's #
8438   *tola'at*

and blue, and purple, and <u>scarlet</u>, and fine linen, and goats' hair, (Exodus 25:4)

This word can represent the color crimson or the worm "coccus ilicis," which when dried, was ground into a powder and used as a dye for the color crimson. This worm also contains a chemical that is an anti-bacterial agent and was included in the formula for the ashes of the red heifer (Leviticus 14:4) used when someone came into contact with a dead body (a host for bacteria).

Darkness

עֲרָפֶל   Strong's # 6205   *araphel*

And the people stood afar off, and Moses drew near unto the <u>thick darkness</u> where God was. (Exodus 20:21)

There are two words in the Hebrew translated as darkness. The most common is the word *hhoshekh* (Strong's #2822) and means "darkness." The other word is *araphel* and means something more than just darkness. In Exodus 20:21, we read *and Moses approached the araphel where God was.* This darkness is a different darkness and may be alluded to in Exodus 10:21 which is the plague of darkness (*hhoshekh*) that could be felt. We often associate darkness with evil and light with good; but, interestingly, most times God appears in this *araphel*, such as we saw in Exodus 20:21 but also in 2 Samuel 22:10, 1 Kings 8:12, Job 22:13, Psalm 97:2 and other places.

Daytime

יוֹמָם   Strong's # 3119   *yomam*

They meet with darkness in the <u>day-time</u>, And grope at noonday as in the night. (Job 5:14)

This word is derived from the word *yom* (Strong's #3117) meaning "day" which can refer to a twenty-four hour period or daytime. The word *yomam* always refers to the daylight hours, the time between sunup and sundown.

Decrease

חָסֵר

Strong's #
2637

hhaser

and the waters returned from off the earth continually: and after the end of a hundred and fifty days the waters <u>decreased</u>. (Genesis 8:3)

This verb means to decrease in size, amount, authority, dignity or reputation. The first use of this word is for the decreasing of the waters from the flood in Genesis 8:3, 5.

Desire

חֵפֶץ

Strong's #
2656

hhephets

But his <u>delight</u> is in the law of YHWH; And on his law doth he meditate day and night. (Psalm 1:2)

This noun can refer to the desire for an object such as gold or silver or an action that one seeks, such as salvation from a deliverer.

Do

עָשָׂה

Strong's #
6213

asah

"And God <u>made</u> the firmament, and divided the waters which were under the firmament from the waters which were above the firmament: and it was so." (Genesis 1:7)

This very common verb simply means "to do" an action and is used in a wide variety of applications. It is frequently used in the context of "making" something.

Dog

כֶּלֶב

Strong's #
3611

kelev

And the Philistine said unto David, Am I a <u>dog</u>, that thou comest to me with staves? And the Philistine cursed David by his gods. (1 Samuel 17:43)

The Hebrew word *kelev* meaning "dog" is only mentioned 31 times in the Hebrew Bible, but never refers to an actual dog. Some references to dogs are as analogies such as in Psalm 59:6: *They return at evening, they howl like a dog, And go round about the city.* Many references to dogs portray them in a negative light: *His watchmen are blind, they are all without knowledge; they are all dumb dogs, they cannot bark; dreaming, lying down, loving to slumber. Yea, they are greedy dogs which can never have enough* (Isaiah 56:10,11). However, there is another interpretation of this word, which could mean "like a heart," by interpreting the letter *kaph* as the prefix meaning "like," and the noun *lev*, meaning "heart."

Dry ground

יַבָּשָׁה   Strong's # 3004   *yabashah*

And God said, Let the waters under the heavens be gathered together unto one place, and let the <u>dry land</u> appear: and it was so. (Genesis 1:9)

To understand the original Hebraic concrete meaning of English abstract words used in translations of the Bible, it helps to look at the roots of the Hebrew word and other words derived from the same root. For instance, the word "shame" is an abstract word but is related to a "dried up ground." When a lake or pond dries up, all of the organic matter begins to decay and stink, which is the Hebrew word *ba'ash* (Strong's #887), derived from the same root as *yabashah*. The word *bushah* (Strong's #955), also derived from the same root, is translated as "shame," but is Hebraicly understood as something someone does that really "stinks."

Dwell

שָׁכַן   Strong's #
7931   *shakhan*

God enlarge Japheth, And let him <u>dwell</u> in the tents of Shem; And let Canaan be his servant. (Genesis 9:27)

The verb *shakhan* means "to dwell," to stay or sit in one location for an indeterminate duration. Several nouns are derived from this verbal root including *shekhen* (Strong's #7933) meaning a dwelling, *shakhen* (Strong's #7934) meaning a dweller, and *mishkhan* (Strong's #4908) meaning a dwelling place and used frequently in the Hebrew Bible for the "tabernacle," the place God dwells. Another word familiar to many, but not actually a Biblical Hebrew word, is *shekhinah*, the presence of God dwelling within the Temple.

Dwelling

מוֹשָׁב   Strong's #
4186   *moshav*

they saw not one another, neither rose any one from his place for three days: but all the children of Israel had light in their <u>dwellings</u>. (Exodus 10:23)

The noun *moshav* comes from the root *yashav* (Strong's #3427) meaning "to settle." A common formation of a noun from a root is to add the letter "M" to the front of the root. This "M" usually adds the meaning "place" to the root, so *moshav* means "settling place" or "dwelling."

Ear

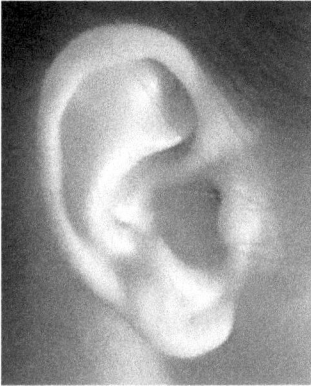

אֹזֶן

Strong's #
241

ozen

"And they gave unto Jacob all the foreign gods which were in their hand, and the rings which were in their ears; and Jacob hid them under the oak which was by Shechem." (Genesis 35:4)

Ozen is the Hebrew word for the "ear" (see Exodus 21:6). A Hebrew's speech is often strange to us, so the translators "fix" the text so that it can be more "modern." However, in some cases the original Hebrew is much more interesting. For instance, in Numbers 11:1, the KJV says "And when the people complained it displeased the LORD." The Hebrew literally reads, *"And the people were murmuring and it was bad in the ear of YHWH."* The verb related to this is *azan* (Strong's #238) meaning "to give an ear" or "to hear." Interestingly, the Hebrew word for a balance is *mozen* (Strong's #3976), derived from *ozen*. Why would a balance be related to the Hebrew word for an "ear?" Could the ancients have understood that a person's inner "ear" included a mechanism for determining balance?

Eysh'dat

אֶשְׁדָת Strong's # 799 *eysh'dat*

And he said, YHWH came from Sinai, And rose from Seir unto them; He shined forth from mount Paran, And he came from the ten thousands of holy ones: At his right hand was a <u>fiery   law</u>   for   them. (Deuteronomy 33:2)

One of the most mysterious words in the Hebrew is the word *eysh'dat*, which only occurs once in the Bible: Deuteronomy 33:2, which states *From [YHWH's] right hand eysh'dat to them.* It has been interpreted by most that this is a combination of two words: *eysh* (Strong's #784) meaning "fire" and *dat* (Strong's #1881) meaning "edict," but because the word *dat* is only used in later Hebrew and *eysh'dat* is written as one word, this interpretation seems unlikely and the original meaning of this word is completely unknown.

Fade

נָבֵל

Strong's #
5034

naveyl

"And he shall be like a tree planted by the streams of water, That bringeth forth its fruit in its season, Whose leaf also doth not <u>wither</u>; And whatsoever he doeth shall prosper." (Psalm 1:3)

This verb means "the fading away" or degradation of a person, action or object. This can be the withering away of a leaf, the wearing out of strength or a non-productive effort.

Fear

יָרֵא
Strong's #
3372

yarey

And he said, I heard thy voice in the garden, and I was <u>afraid</u>, because I was naked; and I hid myself. (Genesis 3:10)

The concrete Hebraic meaning of this verb is "to flow." It is related to the word *yorehh* (Strong's #3138) meaning "first rain" and *ye'or* (Strong's #2975) meaning "stream." When you are seriously afraid of something, you can feel your insides "flowing." This is the meaning of this word that is usually translated simply as "fear."

Feed

רָעָה

Strong's #
7462

ra'ah

"The wolf and the lamb shall <u>feed</u> together, and the lion shall eat straw like the ox; and dust shall be the serpent's food. They shall not hurt nor destroy in all my holy mountain, saith YHWH." (Isaiah 65:25)

The Hebrew verb *ra'ah* means "to feed" and is usually used for the feeding of a flock or herd. The participle form of a verb is formed by adding an "o" after the first letter and an "e" after the second letter. The participle form of the verb *ra'ah* is *ro'eh* and means "one who feeds," a shepherd or herder.

Fire

אֵשׁ

Strong's #
784

eysh

Then YHWH rained upon Sodom and upon Gomorrah brimstone and <u>fire</u> from YHWH out of heaven; (Genesis 19:24)

As the Hebrews were a nomadic people, their lifestyle was much the same as when we go camping, and what camp is not complete without a fire. Not only is it used for camping, but a place where family and friends get together to tell stories, play music and just relax after a long day.

Fish

דָּג   Strong's #
         1709   *dag*

"And the fear of you and the dread of you shall be upon every beast of the earth, and upon every bird of the heavens; With all wherewith the ground teemeth, and all the <u>fishes</u> of the sea, into your hand are they delivered." (Genesis 9:2)

In the original pictographic script used to write Hebrew, and other Semitic languages, this word was written with the picture of a door, the letter *dalet*, representing a "back and forth movement" and the picture of a "foot," the letter *gimel*. When these two letters are combined we have "the back and forth movement of the foot/tail," a perfect image for a "fish." Interestingly, the "a" in the Hebrew word *dag* is pronounced with a short "a" and would therefore be pronounced like our word "dog," another animal with a "tail that moves back and forth." Because of the abundance of fish caught in nets, this word is the origin of another Hebrew word: *dagah* (Strong's #1711) meaning "abundance."

Flesh

בָּשָׂר

Strong's #
1320

basar

within yet three days shall Pharaoh lift up thy head from off thee, and shall hang thee on a tree; and the birds shall eat thy flesh from off thee. (Genesis 40:19)

The word *basar* literally means "meat" such as in Exodus 12:8, but can also mean the whole of a person or animal such as in Genesis 6:13. A closely related word, *besorah* (Strong's #1309), the feminine form of *basar*, means "good news" or "gospel." In the Ancient Hebrew culture, a fatted animal is slaughtered for a feast at times of "good news;" hence, the connection between *basar* and *besorah*.

Flint

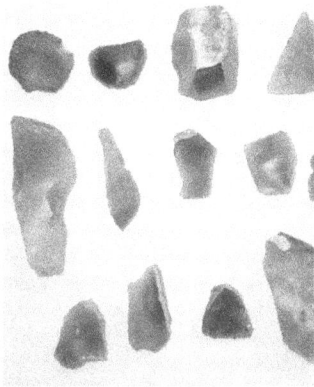

כַּדְכֹד
Strong's #
3539
kad'kod

And I will make thy pinnacles of <u>rubies</u>, and thy gates of carbuncles, and all thy border of precious stones. (Isaiah 54:12)

A flint is a dark colored rock that, when struck with iron, creates sparks. This type of tool has been used since the beginning of man to create fire. A related word, *kiydod* (Strong's #3590) is the Hebrew word for "sparks."

Flute

חָלִיל   Strong's #
2485   *hhaliyl*

And all the people came up after him, and the people piped with <u>pipes</u>, and rejoiced with great joy, so that the earth rent with the sound of them. (1 Kings 1:40)

The Hebrew word *hhaliyl* is an ancient type of flute and comes from the root *hhalal* (Strong's #2490) meaning "to pierce" through, the idea of a "pipe" with holes pierced through it.

Fly

עוֹף   Strong's # 5774   ***ooph***

And God said, Let the waters swarm with swarms of living creatures, and let birds fly above the earth in the open firmament of heaven. (Genesis 1:20)

This verb means "to fly," while the noun form, pronounced *oph* (Strong's #5775) but spelled the same, is a "flyer" and can be a bird, bat or insect, anything that flies. Hebrew commonly uses word puns, words of similar sounds together. Genesis 1:20 is a good example where it says *ve'oph ye'oph* which means "flyers flying."

Form

יָצַר   Strong's #   *yatsar*
            3335

And YHWH God <u>formed</u> man of the dust of the ground, and breathed into his nostrils the breath of life; and man became a living soul. (Genesis 2:7)

This Hebrew verb means to press and form into shape, as a potter does with clay. The participle form of this verb means "potter," as in Isaiah 64:8: "But now, O YHWH, thou art our father; we are the clay, and thou our <u>potter</u>."

Fruit

פְּרִי

Strong's #
6529

p'riy

"And God said, Let the earth put forth grass, herbs yielding seed, and <u>fruit</u>-trees bearing <u>fruit</u> after their kind, wherein is the seed thereof, upon the earth: and it was so." (Genesis 1:11)

The ancient parent root *P.R.* is the origin of the Hebrew word for "fruit," but also for so many of our "fruit" words; PeaR, aPRicot, PRune and PeRsimmon. When reversed we have gRaPe. It is also common for one letter to be exchanged for a similar sounding letter as words are passed from one language to another. One common exchange is the exchange between the R and the L, which adds to the list of "fruit" words coming from the *P.R.* root: apPLe and PLum. Another exchange is the P and B - BeRry and RhuBarb (reversed). The exchange of the P and F brings us back to the word FRuit.

Give

נָתַן

Strong's #
5414

natan

And Abraham ran unto the herd, and fetched a calf tender and good, and <u>gave</u> it unto the servant; and he hasted to dress it. (Genesis 18:7)

This verb is what I call a "generic" verb. While it means to give, it is used in a wide variety of applications. It can mean to set in place, to grant permission, to pay, to speak (give words), to bring forth, to yield and much more.

Glory

כָּבוֹד   Strong's # 3519   *kavod*

"and in the morning, then ye shall see the <u>glory</u> of YHWH; for that he heareth your murmurings against YHWH: and what are we, that ye murmur against us?" (Exodus 16:7)

The word "glory" is an abstract word. If we look at how this word is paralleled with other words in poetical passages of the Bible, we can discover the original concrete meaning of this word. In Psalm 3:3 the *kavod* of Elohiym (God) is paralleled with his "shield," and in Job 29:20, Job's *kavod* is paralleled with his "bow." In Psalm 24:8 we read "who is this king of the *kavod*, YHWH is strong and mighty, YHWH is mighty in battle." The original concrete meaning of *kavod* is "battle armaments." The meaning "armament" fits with the literal meaning of the root of *kavod*, which is "heavy." Armaments are the heavy weapons and defenses of battle. In the Exodus 16:7, Israel will "see" the "armament" of YHWH, the one who has done battle for them with the Egyptians.

Good

טוֹב

Strong's #
2896

tov

And God saw the light, that it was <u>good</u>: and God divided the light from the darkness. (Genesis 1:4)

What is good? From our modern western perspective this would be something that is pleasing to us, but from an Hebraic perspective the Hebrew word *tov*, usually translated as good, means something that is "functional." A complex set of gears in a watch that functions together properly is *tov*. However, if the gears are not functioning properly, then they are *ra* (Strong's #7451), usually translated as "evil" or "bad," but more Hebraicly meaning "dysfunctional." *And God saw everything that he had made, and, behold, it was very good (tov). And there was evening and there was morning, the sixth day.* When God saw his creation, it is not that it was "pleasing" to him; rather, he saw that it functioned properly.

Grab Tightly

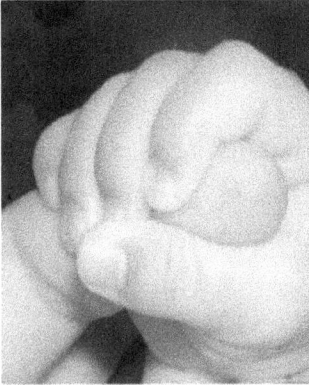

נָשַׁק   Strong's # 5401   ***nashaq***

And his father Isaac said unto him, Come near now, and <u>kiss</u> me, my son. (Genesis 27:26)

The verb *nashaq* means "to grab hold tightly" as when grabbing hold of a weapon for battle, as we see in Psalm 78:9. This same verb can also be used for an embrace, such as we see in Genesis 29:11, where Jacob kisses Rachel.

Gracious

חָנַן   Strong's # 2603   *hhanan*

YHWH make his face to shine upon thee, and be <u>gracious</u> unto thee: (Numbers 6:25)

This verb is often translated as "to be gracious" or "have mercy;" however, these are abstract terms and do not help us understand the meaning of this verb from an Hebraic perspective, which always relates words to something concrete. One of the best tools to use to find the more concrete meaning of a word is to look at how that word is paralleled with other words in poetical passages. In the book of Psalms, the word *Hhanan* is paralleled with "heal," "help," "raise up," "refuge" and "give strength." From a concrete Hebraic perspective, *Hhanan* means all of this and no English word can convey the meaning of the Hebrew, but we could sum up its meaning with "providing protection." Where would a nomadic Hebrew run for protection? The camp, in the Hebrew language, is the word *mahhaneh* (Strong's # 4264), a noun related to *Hhanan*.

Grass

דֶּשֶׁא

Strong's #
1877

deshe

"And God said, Let the earth put forth <u>grass</u>, herbs yielding seed, and fruit-trees bearing fruit after their kind, wherein is the seed thereof, upon the earth: and it was so." (Genesis 1:11)

This word can mean "grass," or other green vegetation, but is also used for the color "green" from the color of grass.

Grave

קֶבֶר

Strong's #
6913

qever

I am a stranger and a sojourner with you. Give me a possession of a <u>burying-place</u> with you, that I may bury my dead out of my sight. (Genesis 23:4)

The grave was commonly a cave owned by the family where its members were laid after death (see Genesis 49:30,31). This is often referred to in the Bible such as in the following verse: *And David slept with his fathers, and was buried in the city of David* (1 Kings 2:10). The verb form *qavar* (Strong's #6912) means "to bury," which is also found in the verse above.

Greece

יָוָן   Strong's #
3120   *yavan*

The sons of Japheth: Gomer, and Magog, and Madai, and Javan, and Tubal, and Meshech, and Tiras. (Genesis 10:2)

For I have bent Judah as my bow; I have made Ephraim its arrow. I will brandish your sons, O Zion, over your sons, O Greece, and wield you like a warrior's sword. (Zechariah 9:13 RSV) The Hebrew name for Greece is *yavan* and is related to the Hebrew word *yayin* (Strong's #3196) meaning wine: The land of wine? *Yavan*, the founder of the land of *yavan*, was the son of Japheth, the son of Noah (Genesis 10:2).

Ground

אֲדָמָה Strong's # 127 *adamah*

"And no plant of the field was yet in the earth, and no herb of the field had yet sprung up; for YHWH God had not caused it to rain upon the earth: and there was not a man to till the ground;" (Genesis 2:5)

Because of the reddish color of soil, this Hebrew word is derived out of the Hebrew parent root *dam* (Strong's #1818) meaning blood. Another word derived from this root is *adom* (Strong's #122) meaning "red" and is also another name for Esau, the brother of Jacob (Genesis 25:30). Another related word is *adam* (Strong's #120) meaning "man," from the blood that runs through his veins, but also because *adam*, the first man, was taken from the *adamah* and his *dam* will return to the *adamah*.

Guide

נָחָה

Strong's #
5148

nahhah

"And it came to pass, when Pharaoh had let the people go, that God <u>led</u> them not by the way of the land of the Philistines, although that was near; for God said, Lest peradventure the people repent when they see war, and they return to Egypt:" (Exodus 13:17)

This verb is closely related to other roots which mean "rest," "quiet" and "comfort." The context of the use of this word in the Bible often implies a guiding or leading of another to a place of rest.

Happy

אֶשֶׁר

Strong's #
835

esher

Blessed is the man that walketh not in the counsel of the wicked, Nor standeth in the way of sinners, Nor sitteth in the seat of scoffers: (Psalm 1:1)

Blessed is the man who does not walk in the council of the wicked (Psalm 1:1). The word "blessed" is the Hebrew word *eher* and has the more concrete meaning of "a cord stretched out straight." One who walks his life "straightly" has a good life or, as we might say, happy. Psalm 1:1 could be better translated as *Happy is the man...*

Heel

עָקֵב   Strong's #
6119   *aqeyv*

and I will put enmity between thee and the woman, and between thy seed and her seed: he shall bruise thy head, and thou shalt bruise his <u>heel</u>. (Genesis 3:15)

This noun comes from the verb *aqav* (Strong's #6117) and means "to grab the heel," meaning "he grabs the heel." From this verb comes the name *ya'aqov* (Strong's #3290) (Jacob, the second born of Isaac) meaning "he grabs the heel." He was given this name because he came out holding onto the heel of his brother Esau. Another word derived from this verbal root is the word *eyqev* (Strong's #6118), which is usually translated as "because," but through the idea of one person doing one thing "on the heels" of another person doing something else. This can be seen in the following verse; *Because (eyqev) Caleb.... followed me fully... I will bring him into the land* (Numbers 14:24).

Herdman

בּוֹקֵר   Strong's #
951   *boqer*

Then answered Amos, and said to Amaziah, I was no prophet, neither was I a prophet's son; but I was a <u>herdsman</u>, and a dresser of sycomore-trees: (Amos 7:14)

Have you ever heard the word "buckaroo?" This was a term from the old west meaning "cowboy," coming from the Spanish word "vaquero." This Spanish word has a relationship with a Hebrew word with the same meaning. The Hebrew word "*boqer*" (sometimes pronounced as *voqer*) means "herdman" or one who works cattle and is derived from the word *baqar* (Strong's #1241) meaning cattle.

Holy

קָדוֹשׁ   Strong's #
6918   *qadosh*

and ye shall be unto me a kingdom of priests, and a <u>holy</u> nation. These are the words which thou shalt speak unto the children of Israel. (Exodus 19:6)

Most of us have certain items in our homes that are used only during special occasion, such as a set of fine china dinnerware or a special suit or dress. Something that is set aside for a special purpose is what is meant by the Hebrew word *qadosh*. The furnishings in the tabernacle were *qadosh* and would never be used for anything but for use in the tabernacle, any more than one would take fine china on a camping trip. The nation of Israel was also *qadosh*; they were set aside from the other nations by God to do his work in the world. The word *qadosh* has been translated as "holy," but this word has taken on a new meaning of its own: a person who is pious and righteous. This is not the true meaning of this word and demonstrates the need for getting back to the original meaning of Hebrew words.

Honey

דְּבַשׁ   Strong's #
1706   *devash*

"He made him ride on the high places of the earth, And he did eat the increase of the field; And he made him to suck <u>honey</u> out of the rock, And oil out of the flinty rock;" (Deuteronomy 32:13)

This word is usually translated as "honey," but literally means "a thick sticky substance" and may refer to honey or dates, a common fruit in the Near East. The phrase *flowing with milk and honey* is probably speaking about a land flowing with milk (probably from the prolific goat herds of the region) and *devash* (honey and/or dates).

Horn

קֶרֶן

Strong's #
7161

qeren

Save me from the lion's mouth;
Yea, from the <u>horns</u> of the wild-
oxen thou hast answered me.
(Psalm 22:21)

The horns of animals were very versatile objects. They were used as trumpets and even as a weapon in war. They were used to store liquids such as olive oil, foods and medicine. In many ancient cultures kings wore horns as a sign of their power; in fact, the points on modern day crowns are holdover representations of horns and, in addition, our word "crown" comes from the Hebrew word *qeren*.

Horse

ס‏וס   Strong's #
5483   *sus*

And the Egyptians pursued, and went in after them into the midst of the sea, all Pharaoh's <u>horses</u>, his chariots, and his horsemen. (Exodus 14:23)

Horses were not a common animal among the nomadic Hebrews, as they were not well suited for the desert. Throughout the Torah (the first five books of the Bible), the only horses mentioned are the horses and chariots of Egypt. In Deuteronomy 17:16 God forbids any future king of Israel from accumulating large numbers of horses by going down to Egypt to acquire them.

House

בַּיִת   Strong's #   ***bayit***
              1004

And there went a man of the <u>house</u> of Levi, and took to wife a daughter of Levi. (Exodus 2:1)

The word *bayit* can mean the "house" the family resides in or the family itself that resides in one "house." This word is also the second letter of the Hebrew *aleph-beyt*. The word "alphabet" comes from the first two Greek letters, alpha and beta, which actually come from the first two Hebrew letters *aleph* and *beyt* (*bayit*), so in Hebrew it is called the *aleph-beyt* rather than the alphabet.

Idol

אֱלִיל

Strong's #
457

eliyl

Turn ye not unto <u>idols</u>, nor make to yourselves molten gods: I am YHWH your God. (Leviticus 19:4)

In Leviticus 19:4 we read, *Do not turn to idols (eliyl) or make for yourselves molten gods* (Leviticus 19:4). An idol is a statue of an image of a god that is believed to have supernatural powers. Such were used by many Semitic peoples living around the Hebrews and by the Hebrews themselves, at times. Interestingly, this word is also used in the following verse, *As for you, you whitewash with lies; worthless (eliyl) physicians are you all* (Job 13:4). An *eliyl* is anything that is considered to have value, but in reality, has no value at all.

Item

כְּלִי

Strong's #
3627

keliy

If a man shall deliver unto his neighbor money or <u>stuff</u> to keep, and it be stolen out of the man's house; if the thief be found, he shall pay double. (Exodus 22:7)

Have you ever counted how many "things" you have in your house? Probably not, but it would easily be in the thousands. We are a culture of pack rats and have items for all kinds of functions (everything from utensils to tools to furniture) and many don't even serve a function (such as knick-knacks). The Hebrew word for an item, any item, is *keliy*. This seems like a pretty broad use of a word, since it could be used for any of the thousands of "things" we have in our homes. But the Ancient Hebrews had very few items and lived very simple lives, so this word would only apply to the few "items" they possessed. The plural form of this word is appropriately translated as "stuff" in Genesis 45:20.

Knife

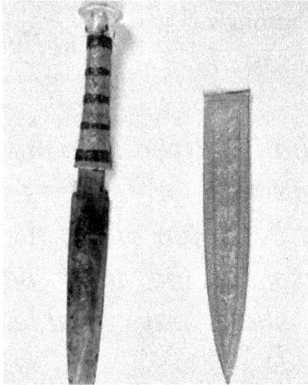

מַאֲכֶלֶת Strong's# 3979 *ma'akhelet*

"And Abraham took the wood of the burnt-offering, and laid it upon Isaac his son. And he took in his hand the fire and the knife. And they went both of them together." (Genesis 22:6)

The Hebrews did not eat with forks or spoons but with knives. The word *ma'akhelet* comes from the root *akhal* (Strong's #398) meaning "to eat." The knife was a very versatile instrument, as it was used in preparing and eating foods, cleaning skins for leather, carving wood or bone and for self-defense. Ancient Knives were made bone, metal, flint or bronze.

Lace

שְׂרוֹךְ

Strong's #
8288

serok

that I will not take a thread nor a shoe-<u>latchet</u> nor aught that is thine, lest thou shouldest say, I have made Abram rich: (Genesis 14:23)

A *serok* is a cord or string that is used to attach the sandal to the foot by twisting it around the foot, ankle and lower leg. This word comes from the verbal root *sarak* (Strong's #8308) meaning "to twist" and is only used twice in the Hebrew Bible, Isaiah 5:27 and in Genesis 14:23, where Abraham refused to owe even a sandal lace to another, a far cry from our credit-driven society of today.

Lamp

נֵר

Strong's #
5216

ner

And thou shalt make the <u>lamps</u> thereof, seven: and they shall light the <u>lamps</u> thereof, to give light over against it. (Exodus 25:37)

A *ner* is an object that gives off light. A common style of ancient lamps was made from clay, had a reservoir for oil and a lip or hole on the edge for the wick. The wick absorbed the oil and the gas coming off the wick was lit giving light. The *menorah* (Strong's #4501) of the tabernacle was a *ner*; in fact, notice that the word *NeR* is found within the word *meNoRah*.

Lead

נָהַל

Strong's #
5095

nahal

He maketh me to lie down in green pastures; He <u>leadeth</u> me beside still waters. (Psalm 23:2)

This Hebrew verb is commonly translated as "to lead" or "to rest," but the more literal meaning of this word is a combination of both of these ideas: "to lead one to a place of rest."

Leaf

עָלֶה

Strong's #
5929

aleh

"And he shall be like a tree planted by the streams of water, That bringeth forth its fruit in its season, Whose leaf also doth not wither; And whatsoever he doeth shall prosper." (Psalm 1:3)

The verbal root word *alah* (Strong's #5927) (different spelling of the Arabic word *allah*) means "to go up" or "to be high." From this root comes the word *aleh* meaning "high" and is used for the leaves of a tree which are up high in the tree.

Leviathan

לִוְיָתָן

Strong's #
3882

leev'yatan

Canst thou draw out <u>leviathan</u> with a fishhook? Or press down his tongue with a cord? (Job 41:1)

Most Bible dictionaries identify this "creature" as a crocodile, whale or snake. However, in Job 41 we are given a detailed description of him, his great size and fire and smoke that come from his nose and mouth and the impenetrable armor of his skin. The best word to describe this creature is a "dragon." It has been speculated by some, and I would agree with them, that this is a large and ferocious dinosaur.

Light

אוֹר   Strong's #
216   *or*

*And God said, Let there be
light: and there was light.*
(Genesis 1:3)

Probably the most quoted passage in the Bible is "Let there be Light." In Hebraic thought, light is associated with order (notice the Hebrew word *or* in the English word *or*der). Genesis 1:3 can be interpreted as "Let there be order" which poetically corresponds with verse 2 that states that the creation was in "chaos."

Lightning

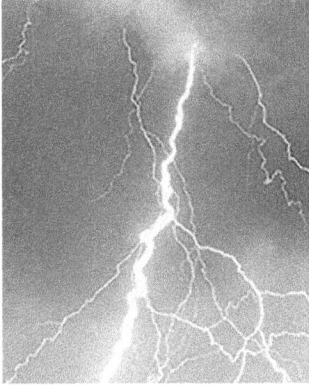

בָּרָק

Strong's #
1300

baraq

"And it came to pass on the third day, when it was morning, that there were thunders and <u>lightnings</u>, and a thick cloud upon the mount, and the voice of a trumpet exceeding loud; and all the people that were in the camp trembled." (Exodus 19:16)

This word means "a flash of light" and is used for lightning, but also for the glistening of a metal weapon such as a sword (Deut 32:41) or spear (Nahum 3:3). In Psalm 144:6 lightning, through Hebrew parallelism, is seen as God's arrows.

Lord

אָדוֹן

Strong's #
113

adon

And Sarah laughed within herself, saying, After I am waxed old shall I have pleasure, my <u>lord</u> being old also? (Genesis 18:12)

The Hebrew word *adon* is "one who has authority over another" or as it is usually translated, a "lord" and is used in the Bible for both men and God. However, from a Hebraic perspective, a "lord" is not one who simply rules over another, but rather one who provides for and protects those under his charge. At this point, a little Hebrew grammar is in order to help understand what the Hebrew behind the word "Lord" really means.

LORD

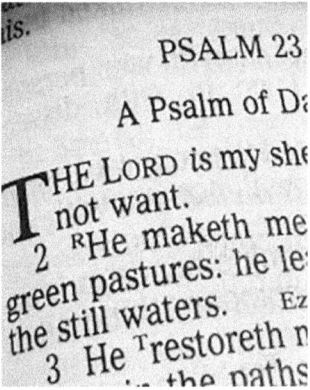

יהוה

Strong's #
3068

YHWH

These are the generations of the heavens and of the earth when they were created, in the day that <u>YHWH</u> God made earth and heaven. (Genesis 2:4)

Virtually all translations from Judaism and Christianity use "the LORD" for the Hebrew name of God: *YHWH*. The original pronunciation of the name can never be determined with complete accuracy, but in Hebraic thought, it is the meaning of a name that is more important than its pronunciation. The Hebrew *YHWH* is the verb *hawah* meaning "to exist" with the prefix *y* meaning "he." Therefore, the word *YHWH* means "he exists." *YHWH* is the one who exists everywhere every time.

Love

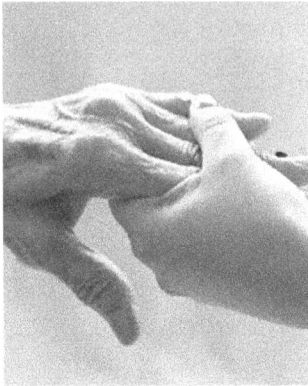

אָהַב   Strong's #   *ahav*
         157

and thou shalt <u>love</u> YHWH thy God with all thy heart, and with all thy soul, and with all thy might. (Deuteronomy 6:5)

We do not choose our parents or siblings, but instead they are given to us as a gift from above, a privileged gift. Even in the ancient Hebrew culture, one's wife was chosen. It is our responsibility to provide and protect that privileged gift. In our modern Western culture love is an abstract thought of emotion, how one feels toward another, but the Hebrew meaning goes much deeper. As a verb, this word means "to provide and protect what is given as a privilege" as well as "to have an intimacy of action and emotion". We are told to love Elohiym and our neighbors, not in an emotional sense, but in the sense of our actions.

Man

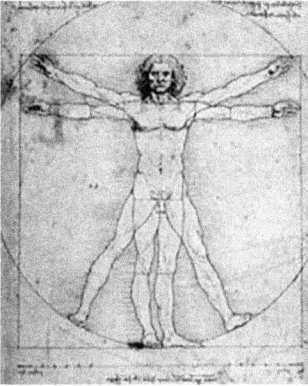

אִישׁ

Strong's #
376

iysh

And the man said, This is now bone of my bones, and flesh of my flesh: she shall be called Woman, because she was taken out of Man. (Genesis 2:23)

A Hebrew word is closely related to its root as well as to other words derived from that root. So, by looking at the root of the word *iysh*, we can gain a clearer picture of the meaning of this word. The root of this word is *anash* (Strong's #605) (the letter n (nun) is frequently dropped from a root) and its meaning can be found in Jeremiah 15:18: *Why is my pain unceasing, my wound incurable, refusing to be healed? Anash* means "to be incurable" like a wound that refuses to heal. This connection between incurableness and man is probably derived from man's mortality. I have heard it said before, "We are born terminally ill," since death is inevitable for all of us.

Meadow

נָאָה   Strong's #
4999   *na'ah*

He maketh me to lie down in green <u>pastures</u>; He leadeth me beside still waters. (Psalm 23:2)

A place of habitation for many animals, wild and domesticated. This word is related to the idea of beauty in the sense that the meadow or pasture is a delightful place.

Milk

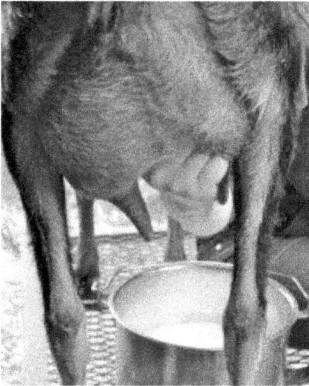

חָלָב   Strong's #
         2461   *hhalav*

And he took butter, and <u>milk</u>, and the calf which he had dressed, and set it before them; and he stood by them under the tree, and they did eat. (Genesis 18:8)

Goats are frequently raised by the nomadic peoples of the modern and ancient Near East. One product from the goats is their milk, a common food staple. This word is also related to the word *hhelev* (Strong's #2459) meaning fat, because of the high fat content in goat's milk. The milk was also turned into cheese, or more correctly curds, by separating out the water in the milk.

Mimic

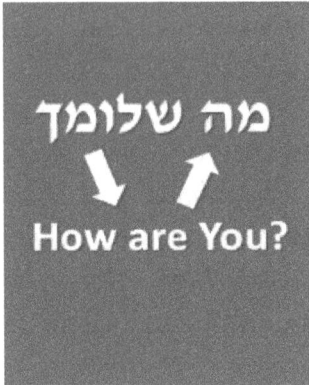

לוּץ   Strong's #
3887   *luts*

A trespass-offering <u>mocketh</u> fools; But among the upright there is good will. (Proverbs 14:9)

This verb means "to repeat or imitate another person's speech as an ambassador, interpreter or mocker."

Mutter

הָגָה Strong's # 1897 *hagah*

And when they shall say unto you, Seek unto them that have familiar spirits and unto the wizards, that chirp and that <u>mutter</u>: should not a people seek unto their God? on behalf of the living should they seek unto the dead? (Isaiah 8:19)

This word is frequently associated with the speaking or muttering of the mouth such as in Psalm 37:30 - *The mouth of the righteous <u>mutter</u> wisdom.* This is not a speaking to another but to one's self, to meditate.

New Moon

חֹדֶשׁ   Strong's # 2320   *hhodesh*

"And David said unto Jonathan, Behold, to-morrow is the new moon, and I should not fail to sit with the king at meat: but let me go, that I may hide myself in the field unto the third day at even." (1 Samuel 20:5)

In Ancient Israel the first crescent of the new moon marked the first day of the month. For this reason, the word *hhodesh* can mean the "new moon" and it is also the word for "month." The related words *hhadash* (Strong's #2319) (masculine) and *hhadashah* (Strong's #2319) (feminine) mean "new" or "renewed" and the verb *hhadash* (Strong's #2318) means to "make new" or "renew."

Night

לַיְלָה

Strong's #
3915

laylah

And God called the light Day, and the darkness he called <u>Night</u>. And there was evening and there was morning, one day. (Genesis 1:5)

Just as the English word "night" means the dark hours of the day, so does the Hebrew word *laylah*. This word is related to other words meaning "to roll back," because the sun is rolling back for its return to its rise in the east.

Nose

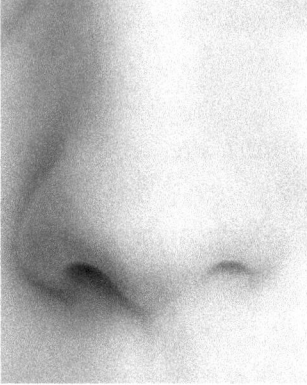

אַף

Strong's #
639

aph

Shall any take him when he is on the watch, Or pierce through his <u>nose</u> with a snare? (Job 40:24)

The Hebrew word *aph* is an excellent example of how a word can be used in a literal and figurative way. *Aph* is literally "a nose," but also is used figuratively as "anger," for an angry person flares his nostrils. This also demonstrates how an abstract concept (anger) is related to a picture of action, unlike modern languages where abstract words are commonly used with no connection to the concrete.

Not

לֹא

Strong's #
3808

lo

Thou shalt <u>not</u> take the name of YHWH thy God in vain; for YHWH will not hold him guiltless that taketh his name in vain. (Exodus 20:7)

The word *lo* means "no" or "not" but is most commonly used to negate a verb. For instance, the verb *asah* (Strong's #6213) is translated as "he did" but *lo asah* would be translated as "he did not."

One

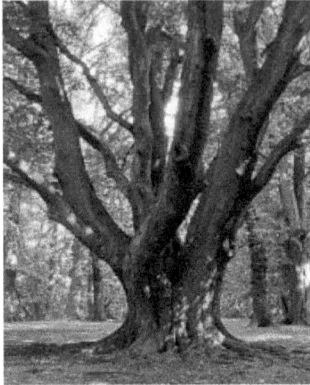

אֶחָד   Strong's # 259   *ehhad*

Therefore shall a man leave his father and his mother, and shall cleave unto his wife: and they shall be <u>one</u> flesh. (Genesis 2:24)

The word *ehhad* is often used for "one," but can also be translated with the word "unit," something that is part of the whole, a unit within a community. In the Hebrew mind everything is, or should be, a part of a unity. There is not one tree, but a tree composed of units within the unity: roots, trunk, branches and leaves. A tree is also in unity with the other trees: the forest. A son is a unit within the brotherhood and the family.

Ox

אֶלֶף

Strong's #
504

eleph

All sheep and <u>oxen</u>, Yea, and the beasts of the field, (Psalm 8:7)

The ox was the "workhorse" of the Ancient Hebrews. Because of its strength, it was used for pulling heavy loads and plowing fields. Another Hebrew word, *eleph* (Strong's #505), is spelled and pronounced identically and means a "thousand" in the sense of mightiness from the idea of the strength of the *eleph*.

Palm Leaf

כִּפָּה   Strong's #
3712   *kippah*

It shall be accomplished before his time, And his <u>branch</u> shall not be green. (Job 15:32)

Because of the palm leaf's shape like that of a hand's "palm," the Hebrew word *kippah* comes from the Hebrew word *kaph* (Strong's #3709) meaning "palm." The word *kippah* is also the modern Hebrew word for the head covering worn by Jews, often called a *yarmulke* (the Yiddish word for a *kippah*), because of its bent shape like a palm.

Pass Through

עָבַר

Strong's #
5674

avar

"For I will <u>go through</u> the land of Egypt in that night, and will smite all the first-born in the land of Egypt, both man and beast; and against all the gods of Egypt I will execute judgments: I am YHWH." (Exodus 12:12)

The Hebrew verb *avar* means to "pass through," such as on a road through a region or to "cross over" a river to reach the other side. The proper name Eber is also this same three letter word with the same meaning: "to pass through" or "one who passes through." The word *eevriym* ^(Strong's #5680) is the plural form meaning "Hebrews" and literally means "ones from Eber" or "ones who pass through." The first person in the Bible identified as a Hebrew is Abram and in Genesis 12:6 we read that Abram *"passed through the land (avar)."* The word *eevriyt*, not used in the Biblical text, is the language of the *eevriym*.

Pasture

מִרְעֶה   Strong's # 4829   *mireh*

And they went to the entrance of Gedor, even unto the east side of the valley, to seek <u>pasture</u> for their flocks. (1 Chronicles 4:39)

The word *mireh* is literally a "feeding place" and is derived from the verbal root *ra'ah* (Strong's #7462) meaning "to feed." The participle form of this verb is *ro'eh*, meaning "one who feeds" or "shepherd."

Path

דֶּרֶךְ   Strong's #
1870   ***derekh***

*"So he drove out the man; and
he placed at the east of the
garden of Eden the Cherubim,
and the flame of a sword which
turned every way, to keep the
<u>way</u> of the tree of life."*
(Genesis 3:24)

A path is a well-marked road or trail that may be
followed to lead one to a specific location. Throughout
the Hebrew Bible, the word "path" is used for man's
journey through life. The path that is followed may be
one that has been carved out by other men or by God.

Peace

שָׁלוֹם

Strong's # 7965

shalom

But thou shalt go to thy fathers in <u>peace</u>; thou shalt be buried in a good old age. (Genesis 15:15)

When we hear the word "peace," as this word is usually translated, we usually associate this to mean an absence of war or strife. However, the Hebrew word *shalom* has a very different meaning. The verb form of the root word is *shalam* and is usually used in the context of "making restitution." When a person has caused another to become deficient in some way, such as a loss of livestock, it is the responsibility of the person who created the deficiency to restore what has been taken, lost or stolen. The verb *shalam* literally means "to make whole or complete." The noun *shalom* has the more literal meaning of "being in a state of wholeness," or "being without deficiency." The Biblical phrase *shalu shalom yerushalayim* (pray for the peace of Jerusalem) is not speaking about an absence of war (though that is part of it), but that Jerusalem, and by extension all of Israel, be complete and whole, and goes far beyond the idea of "peace".

Pen

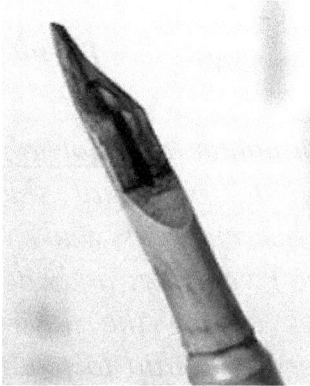

עֵט

Strong's #
5842

eyt

How do ye say, We are wise, and the law of YHWH is with us? But, behold, the false <u>pen</u> of the scribes hath wrought falsely. (Jeremiah 8:8)

Ancient pens were made from reeds where one end was shaved down to form the writing part of the implement. The pen was dipped in ink for writing on papyrus or skins.

Pharaoh

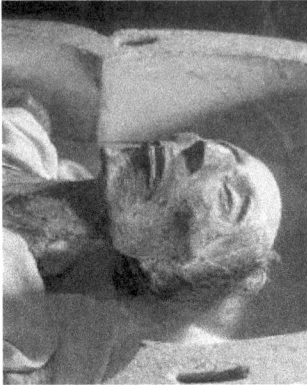

פַּרְעֹה
Strong's #
6547
paroh

"And the daughter of <u>Pharaoh</u> came down to bathe at the river; and her maidens walked along by the river-side; and she saw the ark among the flags, and sent her handmaid to fetch it." (Exodus 2:5)

The Hebrew pronunciation of this word is *par-oh*, unless the previous Hebrew letter, as a prefix or the final letter of the previous word, is a vowel, then it is *phar-oh*. It is believed that this is an Egyptian word meaning "great house." The Egyptian Paroh is also referred to as a king, *melek* (Strong's #4428) in the Hebrew Bible. The pronunciation "pharaoh" actually comes from the ancient Greek translation called the *Septuagint* (*LXX*). In 1974 the mummy of Ramses II was deteriorating and needed to be flown from the Cairo Museum to Paris. Did you know that even a mummy needs a passport? Ramses II was issued an Egyptian passport that listed his occupation as "King (deceased)."

Plow-point

אֶת

Strong's #
855

eyt

"And he will judge between the nations, and will decide concerning many peoples; and they shall beat their swords into plowshares, and their spears into pruning-hooks; nation shall not lift up sword against nation, neither shall they learn war any more. " (Isaiah 2:4)

The metal plow-point was attached to the plow to cut furrows, as marks, in the soil. The two Hebrew letters in this word are the *aleph* and the *tav*, and in the original pictographic script, the *aleph* was a picture of an ox head, the plow puller, and the *tav* a cross, representing a mark: The Ox of the mark. This same word, but never translated, is used over 7,000 in the Hebrew Bible, as a grammatical tool to identify the direct object of a verb. For instance, Genesis 1:1 reads "In the beginning God created *eyt* the heavens and the *eyt* the earth" where the words "heavens" and "earth" are the direct object of the verb *bara* (Strong's #1254) meaning "created." Think of this grammatical tool as a plow cutting a furrow to connect the verb with its direct object. This word is also uniquely spelled with the first (aleph) and last (tav) letters of the Hebrew alphabet: the beginning and the end.

Pounce

עִיט

Strong's #
5860

iyt

"and the people flew upon the spoil, and took sheep, and oxen, and calves, and slew them on the ground; and the people did eat them with the blood." (1 Samuel 14:32)

The fuller meaning of this word is "a bird of prey" (which is the noun *ayit* (Strong's #5861) and is related to *iyt*) that "swiftly falls down onto its prey" (the noun *aht* (Strong's #5706) but, written defectively in the Bible as *ahd*, is also related to *iyt*), tightly grabbing hold of it with its talons to squeeze the life out of it. Notice this imagery in 1 Samuel 14:32 *and the people "pounced" the plunder and took the sheep and the cattle...*

Prosper

צָלַח   Strong's #
6743   ***tsalahh***

"And he shall be like a tree planted by the streams of water, That bringeth forth its fruit in its season, Whose leaf also doth not wither; And whatsoever he doeth shall <u>prosper</u>." (Psalm 1:3)

This verb means "to succeed by advancing forward in position, possessions or action." This word is often used in the context of a successful mission such as we see with Abraham's servant going to his master's homeland for a wife for his son (Genesis 24:40).

Proverb

מָשָׁל   Strong's #
4912   *mashal*

"And he took up his <u>parable</u>, and said, From Aram hath Balak brought me, The king of Moab from the mountains of the East: Come, curse me Jacob, And come, defy Israel." (Numbers 23:7)

A ruler is someone or something that defines a standard of measure. This can be a stick with incremental lines on it for measuring or a person who defines the standard by which people live. The Hebrew verb meaning "to rule" is *mashal* and, when used in the participle form, it means "a ruler," or "one who rules." (Possibly the origin of our word marshal?) The noun form, also pronounced *mashal*, is a parable or proverb. The function of a parable or proverb is to define a standard of measure that one is to live by. For example, *In all thy ways acknowledge him, And he will direct thy paths* (Proverbs 3:6).

Psalm

מִזְמוֹר

Strong's #
4210

mizmor

{To the chief Musician, A Psalm of David.} Deliver me, O LORD, from the evil man: preserve me from the violent man; (Psalm 140:1, KJV)

The verbal root *zamar* (Strong's #2167) means "to make music by 'plucking' a musical instrument." Music or melody is the Hebrew noun *mizmor* and is the word for a Psalm, a song accompanied by a stringed musical instrument. The verbal root *zamar* also means to "pluck" fruit.

Ram

אַיִל

Strong's #
352

ayil

"And Abraham lifted up his eyes, and looked, and behold, behind him a <u>ram</u> caught in the thicket by his horns. And Abraham went and took the <u>ram</u>, and offered him up for a burnt-offering in the stead of his son." (Genesis 22:13)

This Hebrew word is usually translated as "a ram," but also as "an oak tree." Because our modern western minds associate an object with an image, we cannot comprehend how the Ancient Hebrew/Eastern mind saw these two objects as being similar. The Ancient Hebrews associated an object with its function rather than its appearance. The functional meaning of *ayil* is "a strong one;" the ram is the strong one of the herd and the oak, the hardest of woods, is the strong one of the forest.

Reed

סוּף

Strong's #
5488

suph

"And when she could not longer hide him, she took for him an ark of bulrushes, and daubed it with slime and with pitch; and she put the child therein, and laid it in the flags by the river's brink." (Exodus 2:3)

Reeds commonly grow on the banks of rivers. This word is used in Exodus 2:3 for the reeds that were on the edge of the Nile. This word is also the name of the sea that Moses parted, the *Yam Suph*, which translates to the "Reed Sea" but mistakenly is called the "Red Sea." Reeds were used for making twine, rope, baskets and paper.

Rejoice

גִּיל

Strong's #
1523

giyl

That I may show forth all thy praise. In the gates of the daughter of Zion I will <u>rejoice</u> in thy salvation. (Psalm 9:14)

A very common song from the book of Psalms is *This is the day which the LORD has made; let us rejoice and be glad in it* (118:24). "Rejoice" is an abstract word, a Greek form of thought. The Hebrew word *giyl*, translated as "rejoice" in the above verse, is related to other Hebrew words like *galgal* (Strong's #1534) meaning "a wheel," *galal* (Strong's #1556) meaning "to roll" and *galiyl* (Strong's #1550) meaning "a turning." Each of these words is related to "going around in a circle." From a Hebraic concrete perspective "rejoicing," *giyl*, means "to spin around in circles."

Religion

אֹרַח

Strong's #
734

orahh

Now Abraham and Sarah were old, and well stricken in age; it had ceased to be with Sarah after the <u>manner</u> of women. (Genesis 18:11)

One word that is probably most associated with the Bible is "religion." In reality there is no Biblical Hebrew word for religion and you will never find the word religion in any translation of the Hebrew Bible (Tenakh/Old Testament). To the Ancient Hebrews, their religion was their lifestyle and covered all aspects of life from worship to using the latrine (see Deuteronomy 23:13,14). The Hebrew word *orahh* can mean a path used by travelers, as well as the path of life, a lifestyle.

Repeat

עוֹד

Strong's #
5749

ud

"But if the ox was wont to gore in time past, and it hath been <u>testified</u> to its owner, and he hath not kept it in, but it hath killed a man or a woman, the ox shall be stoned, and its owner also shall be put to death." (Exodus 21:29)

This verb means "to witness" in the sense of a person "repeating" what he heard or saw. The noun derived from this verb is *eyd* (Strong's #5707] which is a "witness." Another word coming from this verb is the adverb *od* (Strong's #5751] meaning "again."

Resting

מְנוּחָה Strong's# 4496 *menuhhah*

for ye are not as yet come to the rest and to the inheritance, which YHWH thy God giveth thee. (Deuteronomy 12:9)

The Hebrew verb *nu'ahh* (Strong's #4496) means "to rest." The noun form of this word is *no'ahh* meaning a "resting" and is also the Hebrew form of the name Noah. By adding the "ah" suffix (the feminine ending) and the "m" prefix, a common addition to a root to form another noun, the word *menuhhah* is formed and means a "resting place" or "place of rest."

Righteous

צַדִּיק   Strong's # 6662   *tsadiyq*

Therefore the wicked shall not stand in the judgment, Nor sinners in the congregation of the righteous. (Psalm 1:5)

The Hebrew language is a very concrete language, meaning that each word is a description of an action of a person or object. This is unlike our modern languages that are abstract words. The word "righteous" is an example of an abstract: that has no connection to something physical. The Hebrew word *tsadiyq* does not mean "righteous" in an abstract way, but in the action of staying on course or following the path.

River

נָהָר

Strong's #
5104

nahar

And a <u>river</u> went out of Eden to water the garden; and from thence it was parted, and became four heads. (Genesis 2:10)

A river was considered a giver of life to the inhabitants of the Ancient Near East. Not only did it provide water to the desert, but its annual flooding deposited water in the surrounding land for the production of crops. For this reason, the Hebrew word *nahar* can be translated as "a river" or "a flood."

Rock

צוּר   Strong's #   *tsur*
6697

"Behold, I will stand before thee there upon the rock in Horeb; and thou shalt smite the rock, and there shall come water out of it, that the people may drink. And Moses did so in the sight of the elders of Israel." (Exodus 17:6)

The Hebrew word *tsur* word is used 78 times in the Biblical text and is usually translated as "rock," but means something more than just a rock. This is a large rock outcropping that can be used as a defensive position, a stronghold or fortress. *With God is my salvation and my glory: The rock (tsur) of my strength, and my refuge, is in God.* (Psalm 62:7). A related word, *matsur*, is usually translated as "a fortress."

Sabbath

שַׁבָּת   Strong's #   *shabbat*
              7676

Remember the <u>sabbath</u> day, to keep it holy. (Exodus 20:8)

The verb form of this word is *shavat* ^(Strong's #7673) and literally means "to cease" or "stop." It is first used in Genesis 2:2 where God "ceased" from his work. As ceasing from work is associated with resting, some translate *shavat* as "rest." The noun form is the word *shabbat* and means "a ceasing" or "stopping" and is usually translated as Sabbath, the day God set aside for "resting" from our work (Exodus 20:10).

Sack

שַׂק

Strong's #
8242

saq

"Then Joseph commanded to fill their vessels with grain, and to restore every man's money into his <u>sack</u>, and to give them provisions for the way: and thus was it done unto them." (Genesis 42:25)

Isn't it interesting that the Hebrew word *saq* means sack? Because so many Hebrew words are similar to English, or should I say so many English words "come from" Hebrew, it helps to associate Hebrew words with English when learning the vocabulary.

Scroll

סֵפֶר

Strong's #
5612

sepher

This is the <u>book</u> of the generations of Adam. In the day that God created man, in the likeness of God made he him; (Genesis 5:1)

Books are a fairly recent invention. In ancient times texts were written down on square sheets of skin or papyrus (made from reeds and the origin of our word paper). Multiple sheets would then be sown together creating one long sheet called a scroll. This long sheet was then rolled up and placed in a leather sleeve or clay jar for storage. In caves near the Dead Sea in Israel hundreds of these scrolls were discovered, which included texts of the Tenakh (Old Testament) as well as non-Biblical texts.

Season

עֵת

Strong's #
6256

eyt

then I will give your rains in their <u>season</u>, and the land shall yield its increase, and the trees of the field shall yield their fruit. (Leviticus 26:4)

This word more specifically means "an appointed time" such as a season, a scheduled event, or simply a specific point in time.

Send

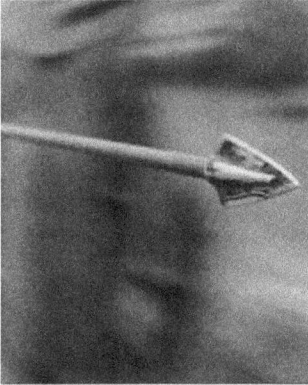

שָׁלַח   Strong's # 7971   *shelahh*

Come now therefore, and I will send thee unto Pharaoh, that thou mayest bring forth my people the children of Israel out of Egypt. (Exodus 3:10)

The Hebrew verb *shelahh* is used over 861 times in the Hebrew Bible and means "to send" in a wide variety of applications such as "to shoot," "cast out," "stretch out," "send away," "throw," "go" and others. Several nouns are derived from this verbal root including *shelahh* (Strong's #7973) meaning a projectile, through the idea of "sending," *shilu'ahh* (Strong's #7964) meaning a present which is sent to another and *shul'hhan* (Strong's #7979), meaning a table where food is sent.

Settle

יָשַׁב
Strong's #
3427
yashav

And Adah bare Jabal: he was the father of such as <u>dwell</u> in tents and have cattle. (Genesis 4:20)

Yashav can mean to settle down in a dwelling for the night or for long periods of time. This verb can also mean to simply sit down.

Shadow of death

צַלְמָוֶת   Strong's# 6757   ***tsalmavet***

Let darkness and the <u>shadow of death</u> claim it for their own; Let a cloud dwell upon it; Let all that maketh black the day terrify it. (Job 3:5)

The Hebrew language rarely includes compound words (two words put together to form one word). One of those few compound words in Hebrew is *tsalmavet*, a combination of the word *tsal* (Strong's #6738) meaning "shadow" and *mavet* (Strong's #4194) meaning "death." The "shadow of death" is despair, danger or tragedy that is understood as a deep impenetrable darkness.

Sheqel

שֶׁקֶל   Strong's #   *sheqel*
           8255

My lord, hearken unto me. A piece of land worth four hundred shekels of silver, what is that betwixt me and thee? Bury therefore thy dead. (Genesis 23:15)

The currency in modern Israel is called a *sheqel* (or shekel). However, in Biblical Hebrew the word *sheqel* was a unit of measurement, a weight of a material such as grain or silver.

Shophar

שׁוֹפָר
Strong's #
7782
shophar

"Then shalt thou send abroad the loud <u>trumpet</u> on the tenth day of the seventh month; in the day of atonement shall ye send abroad the <u>trumpet</u> throughout all your land." (Leviticus 25:9)

Made from a ram's horn, the shofar was used to call an assembly together or an army to battle. The shofar was used in ancient times, as well as in modern times, during the feasts of YHWH and on the Shabbat. In Exodus 19:16, 19:19 and 20:18 the people heard a very loud shofar blast coming from the mountain of God, giving them great fear. This was also the instrument that was sounded when the walls of Jericho fell (Joshua 6:4).

Sinner

חָטָא   Strong's # 2400   *hhata*

Blessed is the man that walketh not in the counsel of the wicked, Nor standeth in the way of sinners, Nor sitteth in the seat of scoffers: (Psalm 1:1)

When one shoots at a target and misses it, we would say that he "missed the mark," just as we see in Judges 20:16: *...every one could sling stones at a hair-breadth, and not miss*. The verb translated as "miss" in this verse is *hhata* (Strong's #2398). This verb is also frequently translated as "sin." God provides man with the target, his teachings, and when man does not hit that target, he "misses the mark." The word *hhata*, the noun form of the verb, means a "sinner," or "one who misses the mark."

Sky

שָׁמַיִם   Strong's# 8064   *shamayim*

In the beginning God created the <u>heavens</u> and the earth. (Genesis 1:1)

There is some debate over the etymology (origins and roots) of this word. The "*sh*" may be a prefix meaning "like" followed by the word *mayim* (Strong's #4325) meaning "water:" like water. It may be the plural form of a noun derived from the verbal root *shamam* (Strong's #8074) meaning "desolate" in the sense of a dry wind blowing over the land, drying it out. It may also be the plural form of the word *shem* (Strong's #8034) meaning "name," but more literally "breath" (in Hebrew thought the name of a person is his breath, since the breath is seen as the character of the individual).

Sling

קֶלַע   Strong's #
7050   *qela*

"So David prevailed over the Philistine with a <u>sling</u> and with a stone, and smote the Philistine, and slew him; but there was no sword in the hand of David." (1 Samuel 17:50)

The sling was a common weapon carried by shepherds to defend the flock; however, modern versions of a sling are very different from those original weapons. The stones were generally 2 to 3 inches in diameter and carefully chipped into a perfect sphere. It was not slung in circles above the head, but slung in one arc in the same manner as a softball is pitched and could be thrown with very surprising force, accuracy and distance. It is a deadly weapon and was used by most all ancient armies of the Ancient Near East.

Son

בֵּן

Strong's #
1121

ben

"Thou shalt betroth a wife, and another man shall lie with her: thou shalt <u>build</u> a house, and thou shalt not dwell therein: thou shalt plant a vineyard, and shalt not use the fruit thereof."
(Deuteronomy 28:30)

In the original pictographic script, the first letter for this was a picture of a tent or house. The second letter was the picture of a seed. The seed is a new generation of life that will grow and produce a new generation; therefore, this letter can mean "to continue." When combined, these two letters form the word meaning "to continue the house." This word is related to the verb *banah* (Strong's #), which means to "build," as one "builds a house" with children. Another related Hebrew word is *even* (Strong's #68), which is "stone," and stones are also used to "build a house."

Stand

עָמַד   Strong's #
5975   *amad*

And the people <u>stood</u> afar off, and Moses drew near unto the thick darkness where God was. (Exodus 20:21)

This verb means "to stand" but can be used in a wide variety of applications, such as to be erect or upright, to remain or maintain in the sense of standing in one place or to establish or appoint in the sense of being stood in a position. The noun form, *amud* (Strong's #5982), is a pillar which stands firm and tall. Both the verb and noun form can be found in Exodus 14:19: *and the pillar (amud) of the cloud went from before their face, and stood (amad) behind them.*

Star

כּוֹכָב

Strong's #
3556

kokav

"And he brought him forth abroad, and said, Look now toward heaven, and number the <u>stars</u>, if thou be able to number them: and he said unto him, So shall thy seed be." (Genesis 15:5)

Of course we know that stars are extremely large balls of gas trillions and trillions of miles out in space, but how did the Ancient Hebrew perceive the stars? Reading the Bible must be from the Hebrew perspective, not ours. The Hebrews, being nomads, lived in black goat hair tents. The hair fabric had pinholes of light and when looking up at the tent roof, it looked just like the night sky. This is alluded to in Isaiah 40:22: [*God*] *stretcheth out the heavens as a curtain, and spreadeth them out as a tent to dwell in.*

Stone

אֶבֶן

Strong's #
68

ehven

And if thou make me an altar of <u>stone</u>, thou shalt not build it of hewn stones; for if thou lift up thy tool upon it, thou hast polluted it. (Exodus 20:25)

In the land of Israel stones were a common building material. The Hebrew word *even* (stone) is related to several other words, all related to "building." *Banah* (Strong's #1129) is a verb meaning to build. *Bohen* (Strong's #931) is "the thumb," considered to be the builder, as the thumb is necessary for doing any work. *Ben* (Strong's #1121) is the Hebrew word "son," the building stones of the family.

Stork

חֲסִידָה
Strong's#
2624
hhasiydah

Where the birds make their nests: As for the <u>stork</u>, the fir-trees are her house. (Psalm 104:17)

A "stork" shows great kindness to its offspring and it was believed that the offspring showed kindness to the parents by caring for them in their old age. The masculine form of this word, *hhasiyd* (Strong's #2623), often translated as "saint," is one who shows kindness to another. These two words are derived from the verbal root *hhasad* (Strong's #2616) meaning "to show kindness."

Stretch out

רָבַץ

Strong's #
7257

ravats

"Judah is a lion's whelp; From the prey, my son, thou art gone up: He stooped down, he <u>couched</u> as a lion, And as a lioness; who shall rouse him up?" (Genesis 49:9)

This verb means to lie down in a resting position to rest, but can also mean to crouch down in hiding for an ambush.

Stumbling-Block

מִכְשׁוֹל   Strong's# 4383   *mikh'shol*

Thou shalt not curse the deaf, nor put a <u>stumblingblock</u> before the blind; but thou shalt fear thy God: I am YHWH. (Leviticus 19:14)

The Hebrew verb *kashal* (Strong's #3782) means "to topple over." This can occur when a person stumbles over the stones of a building that had toppled over. The noun *mikh'shol* (Strong's #4383) is "a ruin," the stone blocks of a wall or building that has toppled down. These blocks are now removed from their original and functional position and are "out of place," which can be a "stumbling-block" to others. *You shall not curse the deaf or put a stumbling-block [mikh'shol] before the blind* (Leviticus 19:14). This "stumbling-block" is a toppled-over block that has been placed before a person to cause them to topple over as well.

Summit

רֵאשִׁית   Strong's #
7225   *reshiyt*

"All the <u>best</u> of the oil, and all the <u>best</u> of the vintage, and of the grain, the first-fruits of them which they give unto YHWH, to thee have I given them." (Numbers 18:12)

The Hebrew root word *rosh* (Strong's #7218) is "the head of a man." Derived from this root is the word *reshiyt* meaning "a summit," the head of a mountain. Hebrew words for "time" are the same words used for "space." For instance, the word *qedem* (Strong's #6924) means "east," but can also mean "ancient." The word *reshiyt* can also be the head of an event, the beginning. While we are very familiar with Genesis 1:1, *In the beginning*, this should literally be translated as *In the summit* and more probably refers to the importance of the creation story rather than its time frame, for the Ancient Hebrews were not as concerned with time as they were event-oriented.

Swarm

עָרֹב

Strong's #
6157

arov

"Else, if thou wilt not let my people go, behold, I will send <u>swarms</u> of flies upon thee, and upon they servants, and upon thy people, and into thy houses: and the houses of the Egyptians shall be full of <u>swarms</u> of flies, and also the ground whereon they are." (Exodus 8:21)

Have you ever had a fly or other winged bug annoyingly and constantly zip around your head? Imagine millions of them and you have a pretty good idea of what the plague of "flies" was like in Egypt (Exodus 8:24). This word is related to other Hebrew words that mean a "mixture" and "darkness."

Teachings

תּוֹרָה Strong's #
8451 *torah*

Because that Abraham obeyed my voice, and kept my charge, my commandments, my statutes, and my <u>laws</u>. (Genesis 26:5)

One of the most misunderstood words in the Hebrew Bible is the Hebrew word *torah*. This word is usually translated as "law," which by definition is a set of rules and regulations established by a government and are enforced with the threat of fines or imprisonment. However, the word *torah* literally means "teachings," a set of instructions given by a teacher or parent in order to foster maturity, and is enforced with discipline and encouragement.

Tent

אֹהֶל   Strong's #
168   *ohel*

And he went on his journeys from the South even to Beth-el, unto the place where his <u>tent</u> had been at the beginning, between Beth-el and Ai, (Genesis 13:3)

Every nomadic culture around the globe constructs tents based on two basic requirements; environment and available material. The Plains Indians of North America lived in cold environments with deer skins available in large quantity. Their shelter of choice was the tee-pee. The Hebrews constructed tents out of spun goat's hair from their herds. Because of the wind and blowing sand, they constructed low profile tents. The sides could be rolled up to allow for air circulation in the heat of the day, and the black hair absorbed the heat of the day to keep it warmer during the night.

Thanksgiving

תּוֹדָה   Strong's #
            8426   *todah*

Offer unto God the sacrifice of thanksgiving; And pay thy vows unto the Most High: (Psalm 50:14)

The word *todah* comes from the verbal root *yadah* (Strong's #3034) meaning "to throw out *the hands.*" This root is in turn derived from the parent root *yad* (Strong's #3027) meaning "hand." This word is synonymous with the verbal root *halal* (Strong's #1984), usually translated as "praise," as can be seen in the following verse where these two words are used in parallel: *I will praise the name of God with a song, And will magnify him with thanksgiving* (Psalm 69:30). In Modern Hebrew this word is used for "thank you."

Thumb

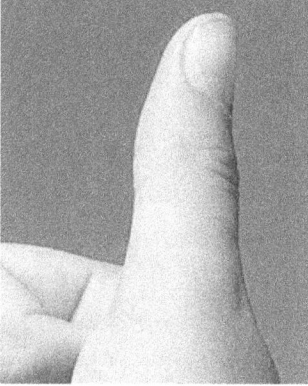

בֹּהֶן

Strong's #
931

bohen

"And he slew it; and Moses took of the blood thereof, and put it upon the tip of Aaron's right ear, and upon the thumb of his right hand, and upon the great toe of his right foot." (Leviticus 8:23)

The thumb was identified as the "builder," because of its need for "work" or "building." This Hebrew word is not only related to the idea of building, but the word *bohen* itself is related to the Hebrew word meaning "to build," *banah* (Strong's #1129).

Title

שֵׁם   Strong's #
8034   *shem*

"and he called his <u>name</u> Noah, saying, This same shall comfort us in our work and in the toil of our hands, which cometh because of the ground which YHWH hath cursed." (Genesis 5:29)

In our modern western culture, a "name" is a series of letters put together to form an abstract identifier of a person. However, in Hebrew, a "name" is more of what we would call a "title," a word with meaning. An example is the "name" *Adam* (Strong's #120) which is related to the Hebrew word *adamah* (Strong's #127) meaning "ground." This link between Adam and ground can be seen in Genesis 2:7 - *And YHWH formed the Adam of dust from the ground.*

Transplant

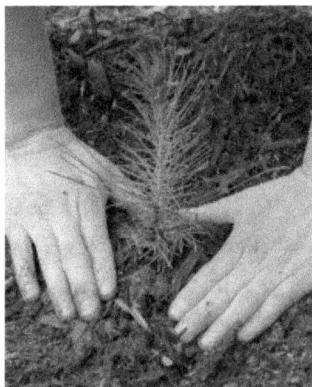

שָׁתַל   Strong's #
8362   *shatal*

"And he shall be like a tree planted by the streams of water, That bringeth forth its fruit in its season, Whose leaf also doth not wither; And whatsoever he doeth shall prosper." (Psalm 1:3)

This verb is almost always translated as "plant," however, this word has the more specific meaning of "transplanting," to remove something from an undesirable location and place it in a desirable location. This can be a plant such as a vine, which is transplanted in better soil or a person who is placed in a better environment.

Tree

עֵץ

Strong's #
6086

eyts

"And out of the ground made YHWH God to grow every tree that is pleasant to the sight, and good for food; the tree of life also in the midst of the garden, and the tree of the knowledge of good and evil." (Genesis 2:9)

When we think of a tree, an image comes to mind; but when the Hebrews, who wrote the Bible, thought of a tree, an action came to mind. This is one of the foundational differences between Ancient Hebrew and Modern Western thought. The Hebrew word *eyts* represents a tree, but embodies more the action of lifting up with support that is the function of the trunk and branches of the tree. Other related words also have this same "active" meaning. The word *atseh* (Strong's #6096) is "the spine," *eytsah* (Strong's #6098) is a "council" and *etsem* (Strong's #6106) is the word for "bones."

Trench

מַעְגָּל   Strong's #
4570   ***magal***

"And David rose up early in the morning, and left the sheep with a keeper, and took, and went, as Jesse had commanded him; and he came to the <u>trench</u>, as the host was going forth to the fight, and shouted for the battle." (1 Samuel 17:20, KJV)

When wagons are repeatedly driven down a path, the wheels cut grooves, ruts or trenches in the path. These grooves force wagons to follow this very same path time after time. For this reason, this word means a path that is well defined and easy to follow.

Tributary

פֶּלֶג

Strong's #
6388

peleg

"And he shall be like a tree planted by the <u>streams</u> of water, That bringeth forth its fruit in its season, Whose leaf also doth not wither; And whatsoever he doeth shall prosper." (Psalm 1:3)

Peleg comes from the verbal root *palag* ^(Strong's #6385) meaning "to split." A tributary is a stream that is "split" off from the main river.

Truth

אֱמֶת

Strong's #
571

emet

Thy righteousness is an everlasting righteousness, And thy law is truth. (Psalm 119:142)

The root of this word is *aman* ^(Strong's #539), a word often translated as "believe," but more literally meaning "support," as we see in Isaiah 22:23 where it says "I will drive him like a peg in a place of support..." A belief in Elohiym is not a mental exercise of knowing that Elohiym exists, but rather our responsibility to show him our support. The word *emet* has the similar meaning of firmness, something that is firmly set in place.

Turn back

שׁוּב

Strong's #
7725

shuv

"in the sweat of thy face shalt thou eat bread, till thou return unto the ground; for out of it wast thou taken: for dust thou art, and unto dust shalt thou return." (Genesis 3:19)

This word means "to return to a previous state or place." The first use of this word is found in Genesis 3:19 where man (*adam*), who is taken from the ground (*adamah*) will return (*shuv*) to the ground (*adamah*). This verb is frequently used for repentance, where one is going in the wrong direction but then turns around and heads back in the correct direction.

Valley

גַּיְא   Strong's #
                1516   *gai*

So we abode in the <u>valley</u> over against   Beth-peor.
(Deuteronomy 3:2)

The parent root of this word is *gey* ^(Strong's #1341), a word meaning "pride" in the sense of lifting oneself up to a high position. The word *gai* is "a valley," a place surrounded by "high" walls. While a valley can be a place of beauty, it can also be a place of darkness and defenselessness.

Vineyard

כֶּרֶם

Strong's #
3754

kerem

And Noah began to be a husbandman, and planted a <u>vineyard</u>*:* (Genesis 9:20)

This word is first mentioned in Genesis 9:20 when Noah planted a vineyard for making wine. One of the oldest and most common fruits grown in the Ancient Near East, the grape was predominately used for making wine. The grapes were also dried and pounded into cakes.

Walk

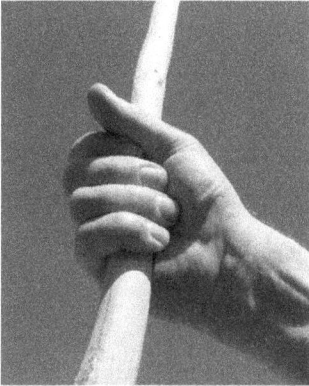

הָלַךְ

Strong's #
1980

halak

Arise, <u>walk</u> through the land in the length of it and in the breadth of it; for unto thee will I give it. (Genesis 13:17)

This word is found over 1300 times in the Bible and can be used in the sense of "going," "coming," "carrying," "bringing," "leaving," "following" and even "walking." The original pictographs used to write this word are a picture of the palm of the hand and a staff. What is one going to do when they put a staff in the palm of the hand? Take a walk.

Wall

חֵיל

Strong's #
2426

hheyl

Peace be within thy <u>walls</u>, And prosperity within thy palaces. (Psalm 122:7)

Many of the cities mentioned in the Bible were surrounded by a large wall to keep an enemy from entering the city. Because an army performs this same protective function, they are also called a "wall," or in Hebrew a *hheyl*. *Hhayil* (a closely related word) is the Modern Hebrew word for the "army" of Israel.

Water

מַיִם Strong's #
4325 *mayim*

And the earth was waste and void; and darkness was upon the face of the deep: and the Spirit of God moved upon the face of the waters. (Genesis 1:2)

This word is first used in the above verse. This Hebrew word is used for any water, whether it is a jar of water or the water of the oceans. A very interesting Hebrew idiom is "water at the feet" meaning "urine" (2 Kings 18:27).

Weave

שָׁבַץ   Strong's # 7660   *shavats*

"And thou shalt <u>weave</u> the coat in checker work of fine linen, and thou shalt make a mitre of fine linen, and thou shalt make a girdle, the work of the embroiderer." (Exodus 28:39)

Weaving means to take several different strands of material and intertwine them together to create an object, such as a basket. A related verb is *hhashav* (Strong's #2803) meaning "to think" or "calculate," which is to take several different ideas and intertwine them to create one primary idea.

Well

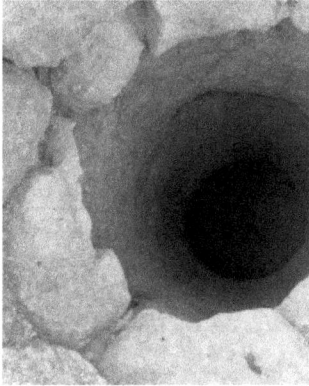

בְּאֵר

Strong's #
875

be'er

Wherefore the <u>well</u> was called Beer-lahai-roi; behold, it is between Kadesh and Bered. (Genesis 16:14)

Ancient wells were holes dug down in the ground to the water table. The well was usually covered over with a large rock to keep debris out and prevent people from falling in. The stone was removed and a bucket tied to a rope was lowered to retrieve the water. As nomads, the Ancient Hebrews knew the locations of many wells in the area of their journeys. City wells were usually inside the city walls, so that its inhabitants had access to water during sieges. Some wells were so large a winding staircase was cut in the sides of the well for people to descend down into the well. In the case of the Siloam well, located outside the city, a tunnel from inside the city to the well was cut through solid rock.

Which

אֲשֶׁר

Strong's #
834

asher

"And God made the firmament, and divided the waters which were under the firmament from the waters which were above the firmament: and it was so." (Genesis 1:7)

The Hebrew word *asher* can be translated as the relative participle "which" or "who(m)." It is derived from the parent root *shar*, meaning a "cord." A cord is used for attaching one thing to another. The word *asher* is related to this idea of attaching one part of a sentence to another, such as we see in Genesis 2:8 - *"the Adam whom he formed.*

Wicked

רָשָׁע

Strong's #
7563

rasha

Blessed is the man that walketh not in the counsel of the <u>wicked</u>, Nor standeth in the way of sinners, Nor sitteth in the seat of scoffers: (Psalm 1:1)

In the English language a wicked person is one who performs evil. However, in the Hebrew language the noun *rasha* has a very different meaning. By investigating the verbal root of this word, we can gain a clearer picture of its meaning. The root of this word is the verb *rasha* ^(Strong's #7561) and its original concrete meaning can be found in Psalm 18:21: *For I have guarded the paths of YHWH, and have not <u>departed</u> from my Elohiym.* (Most translations have "wickedly departed," but the word "wickedly" is added to the text and is not part of the Hebrew). The verb *rasha* means "to depart from the path," either by walking off the path on purpose or by becoming lost from the path. The noun *rasha* is "one who has walked off the path."

145

Wilderness

מִדְבָּר   Strong's #
4057   *mid'bar*

And YHWH said to Aaron, Go into the <u>wilderness</u> to meet Moses. And he went, and met him in the mountain of God, and kissed him. (Exodus 4:27)

For forty years Elohiym had Israel wander in the "wilderness." Insights into why Elohiym had chosen the wilderness for their wanderings can be found in the roots of this word. The root word is *davar* (Strong's #1696) and is most frequently translated as "speak," but more literally means to "order" or "arrange" words. The word *midbar* is a place existing in a perfectly arranged order, an ecosystem in harmony and balance. By placing Israel in this environment, he was teaching them balance, order and harmony.

Wind

רוּחַ   Strong's # 7307   *ru'ahh*

And the earth was waste and void; and darkness was upon the face of the deep: and the <u>Spirit</u> of God moved upon the face of the waters. (Genesis 1:2)

In Hebrew thought the wind can be many things. It is the wind that blows in the sky, it can be the breath of man or animals and it is also the breath of God. In Hebrew thought your breath is your character or essence; it is what makes you, you. The breath, or wind of God, is his character or essence. In the same way that our breath is like a wind, God is like a wind. God is not an individual person that exists as we do; he is everywhere just like the wind is everywhere. Many times the Hebrew word *ru'ahh* is translated as "spirit," but this abstract term takes us away from the real concrete meaning of the Hebrew word. Rather than looking at God as a spirit, we can read the text more Hebraicly if we replace the word "spirit" with "wind."

Wine

יַיִן
Strong's #
3196
yayin

"and thou shalt bestow the money for whatsoever thy soul desireth, for oxen, or for sheep, or for <u>wine</u>, or for strong drink, or for whatsoever thy soul asketh of thee; and thou shalt eat there before YHWH thy God, and thou shalt rejoice, thou and thy household." (Deuteronomy 14:26)

The Hebrew word *yayin* means "wine" and may possibly be the origin of the word "wine." The phrase *"fruit of the vine"* (see Matthew 26:29) is an idiom meaning "wine." The Jewish blessing for the wine is *"barukh atah adonai eloheynu melekh ha'olam borey <u>periy hagafen</u>"* meaning *"blessed are you O Lord our God, creator of the <u>fruit of the vine</u>."*

Woman

אִשָּׁה   Strong's #
802   *ishah*

And the man said, This is now bone of my bones, and flesh of my flesh: she shall be called <u>Woman</u>, because she was taken out of Man. (Genesis 2:23)

The Hebrew word for woman is *ishah*, derived from the masculine noun *ish* (Strong's #376) by adding the "*ah*" suffix, which is often used for feminine nouns. It is interesting to note that just as the word "man" is found in the English word "woman," it is also so in the Hebrew language.

Write

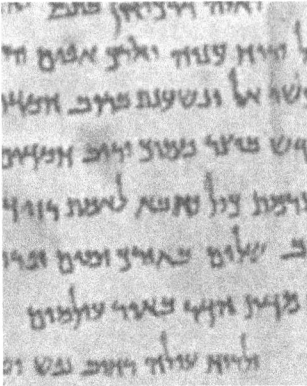

כָּתַב

Strong's #
3789

katav

"And Moses <u>wrote</u> all the words of YHWH, and rose up early in the morning, and built an altar under the mount, and twelve pillars, according to the twelve tribes of Israel." (Exodus 24:4)

Several methods of writing were used in ancient times. Wet clay was written on with a stylus, a pointed stick. Papyrus and leather were written on with reed pens using ink. Rocks were written on with chisels. Wood was written on with sharp objects.

www.ingramcontent.com/pod-product-compliance
Lightning Source LLC
Chambersburg PA
CBHW050013100426
42739CB00011B/2631